Wires
That
Sputter

Wires
That
Sputter

Poems

Britta Badour

McCLELLAND & STEWART

Published simultaneously in the United States of America.

Library and Archives Canada Cataloguing in Publication data is available upon request.

ISBN: 978-0-7710-0454-4
ebook ISBN: 978-0-7710-0455-1

Book design by Talia Abramson
Cover images: Talia Abramson
Typeset in Esta by M&S, Toronto
Printed in Canada

McClelland & Stewart,
a division of Penguin Random House Canada Limited,
a Penguin Random House Company
www.penguinrandomhouse.ca

1 2 3 4 5   27 26 25 24 23

Penguin
Random House
McCLELLAND & STEWART

for Grandma Mary & Cousin Quita

Contents

: WIRES THAT SPUTTER :

: listening for sirens : flashbacks : you split net fluently : you don't live with any bookshelves : you don't school with any kids you look like : but you understand poor punctuation : you've never seen idioms in your image : out of what twisted music you were pushed : what rattles and rico-chets : as necessary as what breathes one hard unaltered spark : there's an atlas you deserve and their hardcover yawn won't fit you

: you get splittability : enjambment is your armour : is freedom : what questions and cusses : what carols you catapult : to a blank page : the possession you resist : whipped : bounced : the golden bed of your ether : namelessness listening : is there

: pressed to ear : headphones : bedroom walls : behind this envying : the last chapter of violent autobiographies : the brittle cleft of dining plates : upheaval of keepsakes like school-day portraits in plastic gold frames : *your bully and your craft* : an illiterate debt : you live and read the arrows inflating your torso : both target and secret : dysfunction your inner voice : you keep a private collection of daydreams and lyrics : you carry whispers not yours to slick : you scratch apologies on yourself : you're an essay written in jazz trumpets and asthmatic lungs : work twice as hard to exhale

: to admit what you call beauty : what you can't say out loud : what you can't hold : down : what you must not put into plain paragraphs : more cussed than a wrinkled grocery bag of tinsel : a strip of grammatic dyna-mite : a certain power you can replenish : out of the contraption you imag-ine yourself : a brilliant and more desirable spin : what you listen for when you are most alone : the quality of voice you speak : to yourself : how care-fully you read

: the fractures of a family you stanza together : the sporadic spell : a piercing memory of what was not meaning : if you reach one lifetime elsewhere : if you expect better for one else : you double : is fuel for self-grasping : the performance of painlessness has failed your family : you are a product and a people : you must personify hidden glaciers to break the fever : to dismantle its grey legacy : your notebook of names for ancestors for painters : experts and self-selected kin : there are new daydreams and lyrics to collect : you keep across the page : despite

: between you : and hard listening : is stolen territory : is grammar : is headquarters : is a world not made : the world you perplex : is celebrating : and maybe sometimes : someplace you don't have to keep affirmations : someplace not programmed by empires : someplace you recognize an abolished hierarchy : a diluted fear : no recessive and abusive patterns to taste you : until then : this current : this constitution swaggers : digs debt : this grammar needs numbers : this cosmetic code : cologne and all-inclusive vacations : this gravity of extraordinary suffering : this desire to misunderstand suffering : to cover the stench : bottled listening : sometimes it asks you to speak on behalf : preservation is not wanting to bother : is not wanting to be bothered : is not tempted to volley weapons in all directions the way flower petals grow : your intelligible slant and slang : here is you : is trinket of choosing : is not going back to serving the way they scripted you

: archaic cadence into obedience : a violent home is no protected wilderness : the grammar is no safer than body : these stadiums : these courtrooms and towns : theatres : clubs and synagogues of bodies : pitied : bracketed : starved : trafficked and attacked : granting bodies : what new grammar you hear them making : follow with a finger : return : punished : are missing : your daydream reaches : sometimes a voice you squeeze through : moves the material : a pen in your hand : you don't tell it what to do

: a whirl : from the first needle on the track : from warm to cool : from biology to : your total loves : all the directions your crown of petals grow : your slant and slang : here is you : new wires that sputter : that speck : that spark : is all you : not going back

: you disrupt architecture : books arch into irises with no rooftops : you keep only what returns to be studied : student to all language : is yawning enough : between your chores : bridged chores : endangered chores : how you rattle *the light of the ear* : in what name you give a future : how you keep across the page

: HURRICANES :

IF YOU START SOME SHIT IN PUBLIC
better never come home

bend all the ways I howl   or be cut
out   baby photos

            don't dare

                    who would

drop this whip? heat? *help*?
                        what help

We   's   be underdogs
We pile deep   hunter green caravan, Summer '94
baby brother mother father nanny and me team   Mac's Milk
chewing tobacco   penny candy   secondhand suitcases
stuffed with K-Mart clothes   fifteen-hour full court
press from Leroy Grant Dr. in Kingston to Perkins St. in Greensboro
We time out in Virginia Beach

     The whole city smells like saltwater taffy. I've got nothing but a
souvenir memory of arguments   if you want something to cry about

I play this scrimmage as a real game   blow elbows into my teammate's
     chest
box out   pivot   dribble   *shoot!* (don't shoot)   keep your
head   hustle the court   pass   possess the ball
take possession of the ball   GET THE BALL   GET THE
BALL   NOW!   GET THAT FUCKING BALL BACK

: *California Dreamin'* :

passing a church. I come home to Ma
mopping "Midnight Train to Georgia" lyrics
in the kitchen all the way to the linen closet.
I figure I've never heard nobody sing
nothing about my hometown
the way feeling alone makes Ma

dim her headlights in the driveway, and sit
in the car for a while. Ma's a white lady.
She got *Everlasting Life* brochures in her purse.
Sometimes at the mall, somebody else's mama
starts to interview me: "Are you here alone?
Where is your—"   Ma socks it to them,

I'm her mother.

The flowerpot of my frame makes it hard for folks
to believe I'm a germ from grey skies and white
roses. Bible studies taught me how to tower,
how to read shoulders—shoulders tell you which way
somebody's going. While Ma delivers paradise

brochures door-to-door, brother and me busk
to make some cash for her gas bill. You can dream Ma
's wintery beauty brush on our baby
brown cheekbones.   We take turns
with our mirrors and flicker
all that white people's paint 'til it dries.

We nod   how in sync.
How we look, how we lip.
Like Sonny and Cher.   Men as old
as rust flip business cards into our piggy banks.
We swear we got it all: all promise and electricity.
Flipping our long wigs from Salvation Army.

Never had nobody tell us different. My eyelashes
fall out like those leaflets in screen doors
but everyone loves ol' mini-Sonny, him
and his fake mustache.   You can dream Ma
's headlights when people make a scripture of us
like a midnight lilting or an aimless little girl

The cartoon man manages other middle-class men. He sits in his office chair, belligerent at every workday clock, the audience never sees him on legs. Chicken grease stains him crumbs his pimples his face. Countless KFC buckets wrap his desk.

Who must want his greed and I, his heinous isolation.

: LETTERS TO MIRANDA :

here we are maybe two and four
here, little girls on an old grey couch
the same length of hair, curly dark brown
the same bathtub and bedtime stories
the same eczema-cracked and cork colour skin
here we are bewildering
our single mothers' make-believe, we sisters
here we are dancing to Boys II Men
here we are maybe four and six and Miranda is leaving
I repeat the alphabet for twenty years
I write letters to Miranda signed to no new address
for twenty years I dream
here I learn last names and fathers can live outside the blood
should I keep these letters   here mom, *here*

: At My Best :

it t'
aches   embr ace

for
grand t'
id

bee   coss it   wandce   toque

tut   *shh!*

bi   thrEDt

my small birdhouse   my curse to combust

end   wen
kno   bod   he is   looking

aye   crush   de   wings

end brake de baeks

mo   awdience   mo   uplawz

mo   warpT
aye want
to   lie   fl-at

kno   bod   he is   looking

kno bod he   hes seen me at my   best

: *Eyeblade I* :

above your eye
I am marked where I am
Where I'm not I've heard
cameras never reveal true portraits

I swig the analog buzz code
They or you-ever say 1990
and I am brackish gallery of hallway carpet
Here in the corner of your grandparent's fifth floor apartment
announced, announcing, I strum a lightning
I ring when I
enter but don't wipe my feet
Is a name given for its face
or for the cleft a face inherits?

there are other symptoms, too
Before bedtime stories
you learn to read temperature, the swelling of light
What gets hit is not as important as what pounds
What shadows you research
from a crack in the door

and memory	persists
and injury	persists
there were fouls there	were emergencies
what you were	not fighting
not for the first time	coward
I have kept	the book
no one could	put me back
I had no	one's face
no one	's
no	benefit

no last name
At the only exit I begin
A claw opening your eye
I wink at your mother, shake her chandeliers
heave your father's sky-scraping voice,
split
the bill at the *good* Denny's
What stories you tell
before you're taught to read

: ONLY BOOK IN THE HOUSE :

Him I traced
Tuesday nights
some Thursday nights
Saturday mornings
and Sundays

Him I followed with my bullet-finger
and could not make glow

He was not mine
but child, I paid attention
Did I have a choice?
I tasted every awful rip in His sleeve

: THINKING 'BOUT PARTS :

what advice would I give
a woman who is
kingdom whose
body is a house
with preludes

my home   a body   of woman and kingdom
and an anxiety about opening photo albums
                              : all them windows have hauled walls :
doors boarded up

                                        must I speak
                                        with barbed wire
                                in my injuries? do I have earth
                        enough to reveal
                                the hurricanes I've kept under
                                        my bed?
my mother never talks about her mother's nature
how her father's fatherhood rephrases intimacy
my mother never lets me have friends in the house
to let anybody meet me
any closer than the curb
must I emerge from the fire escape?

if told *it runs in the family*
does it change the way you chew   if someone swallows the book of
    forgiveness
how do you caution tape that grief   how to keep safe a woman
from that kingdom
you lose control to   control?

what kind of host or bit am I
when your only options
are *do what I tell you to under this roof*   or leave

: IF HIS MAMA :

Having five children of my own to carry
and food stamps on Christmas; how many times
we were robbed and always
had big-bellied fireflies and sweet
tea in the front yard?
Some grief
is good, you know. Watching you drive
away then come back from the Army and forth
like a swing or tsunami and back with my grandbaby
's eyes bragging of cherry blossoms. In May, if asked,
I would've said you'll either have hurricanes
or become one. Goodbye
is a blister no less tender than the driftwood's
capacity to heat. My boy, you must understand
even with no certainty I still cling
to next time.

: Trap Music :

aye wire ah snare

                              aye wire ah sputter

                   aye dip mah scribble in floor-een

an' enywun tutch this

      burns brusque brilly-yoncé

     lawd *y e l l o w* leaves huge
              blues & radish redz

bevor November's inevitable
                   frost ah con-scentrate

                              lak aye squinting

lak aye heaven a real gud time

: BLACK BOOTS :

said no black

and broke in-
to black
boots
loosened the strings of my black, black
hoodie
pulled my head   see-through
soaked black worry
in a bath
of black lafter

tucked into, tinkered out of black
turtleneck fractures
saw the spy
on the other side
of the tunnel
spat purple-black paranoia
over boom bap
stitches hunched
pitch black
helmet hips,
black shellac fists
rolled around in black cotton sheets and t-shirts
'til I snatched
cavities
on a black satin dress
took it off and put on
black track pants
and black leather gloves

felt   my way through   the dark
of a long   black coat's
arms   parked in front of the mirror
with black
wings

of what little I got, I and a lot of blackish
and
black

begin every day
re-entering this
black-   listed   grin

black comes back

black attracts black

black goes
with everything
sure

but what would you give to be
the blackest thing

on earth?

: *Eyeblade II* :

dead set to strip

from belonging

is ownership too much belonging?

could we say you belonged to a weekday?

what work-free day could be afforded
if not for emergency rooms

: eyes study
vibration of floors : the degrees of a door :

after you learned how to put a table back
on its feet you stood

: consequence
: had you known what to say : of voicelessness

did you have birthdays with parties? no, but predict what property
would set on fire and that you could

: *Cuffs or Halo* :

been chemistry   been psyched   been
's peach   been trophied, studied, stolen

                          been faded away

back on earth
you was crusty
coachable humid nosebleed

who be tip-off
who be target
who be bound
                to this hoop this bucket this *slishh* of small suns

                   this catcher's mitt of hard rock parabolas

                   this kingdom of sweat and full-court pressure

summoned and stoned gods lurk from low-income balconies
           who's hood is it anyway? who's house is this?
Who's house?

if I had a dream   I had a halo   ten-feet high

comets slickin' my neon-cuffed neck

                the game played me and I be hustlin' right back

: We Don't Root for the Home Team II :

I am family's vacation unchained, melody my mouth medium rare with a side
of cold fries can you   *catch me some sweet water?*   I've got good defense
handles   *nice tricks, nice tricks*   I've got hard habits   close to the
hoop, maple courts' floorboards   squeak and sneakers ready. Just don't
expect me

to scoop points   I am backboard brick   buckets be embezzled   my
good aim and fade away jumpers' hand in the cookie jar   the moment
the rubber-stippled sphere leaves my secret handshake   insecure
I always   throw each shot with eyes closed   I don't celebrate
shortened tempers but I've

got a soft spot for both teams the wife beaters and the skins   *hurray!* get
overemotional like *The Maury Povich Show* when the man who is not the
father decides to pick the kids up from school anyway   if there's ever
been a bandwagon with my name on it   I was rooting for the visiting team

How about *Kingston Penitentiary*
or *Kingston Police Officer* calmly cards
my crew, he is casually calling for backup
has "a group of non-white males", he spits
Copenhagen blood. How the fuck do you expect me
to not come apart harping on the tar that proves my dad
's a factory worker with *NIGGER* kicked into office door?
Relax, "Jamaica was not my first guess"

but some Sir John A. signage would've helped, *eh*.
White girl sits googling the # of cities called Kingston.
The class bell rings, a private breaking and entry.
When black eyes are suspected but not my own
I am pinched for them anyway, packed into lower jaw
and what they keep me for? How about   you decide.

: Bullet Ant :

AYE

       DIS

              LO   CAY TED

     SYNA   PSE

  AYE THE DIS   LO   CA   TED   SNAP

    ROUTE   B LACK ER   THAN

                            BLUES
                            BROOZED

EGOS   BOW   B   *ow!*

       TO   THE PUR   POSE OR

BE LONG   TO A   PEOP   ULE

    S'POW   ER FUL   HOW

MAN   EEY

  SHOOT

     ING   STARS   WE

             DON'T   COUNT

    IN   'S

    DAY

      LIGHT

: 's BACK AGAIN :

Always on a Monday
In case you thought I forgot

The top of an ice cream
The supreme sprinkle

Braids brim-spilled shoulders
If we were not tired

By the ears of our Cabbage Patch dolls
We swang

We were two toe-tipping time capsules
Stuck in traffic to the kitchen

Squeezing the necks of icing packs
Toaster strudels breaking in two

Half strawberry, half nail polish
And guardians on doorframes

The first memory I have
of having a radio
of twisting the dial
to discover a girl
's voice

buried

in the future
on all these tightropes
I sketch
scribble back to her
to make mine again: but

Every time I've loved
I've loved like I was missing
Like I already attended that funeral
Too fast, too soon

: SONNY'S FOUND POEMS :

after James Baldwin

's hungry world above us
's little girl in trouble
a cup of milk, I ask
's moment, a breath
a lot of applause after
a bluesy chord and my brother
soaking wet, and grinning

The juke box began
It filled everything
Dark, quick

Its icy wings   the corners, the gut of its tune
The almost whispered
I'm—

Pulling the dread I'd felt all afternoon
Killing, cheerfully
I didn't want to go

The spilling out   the swinging lights
The high sometimes
Hardened   sometimes scared

Spilling out
Bright and open
Like now   a private raid inside me

in the shadow
a boy too young, hanged

I don't know why
I hated him

he looked sort of like a cigarette, shaking
a bright sun
a little one

Good boy, my brother
      All that light in his face

Rage dreamed   a long time
I listened, struck
Thinking about my good brother

A boy, an algebra   or a bird
Holding his own

      All that light in his face

              Dear Brother,

        You don't know how much I wanted
               to climb up dead
             Blow my brains for you

            And hurt you so fine
            What good does it do
        to blame me,   's?

In constant cold he came forgotten
This deepened life, the distant
Animal coaxed into light

These years have all but known flooding
Between us, a bridge. A baby
  's opera born:
  Just dying to see you!

A beautiful little fever
in the kitchen fixing lunch.

In the living room in the dark, him
by his-self drinking.

Courage
what he'd do once he found it.

an expired subway ticket that reads:

to roll clear   between his palms
a space between
his hands
to glitter, like a small rose

And that's how he got so goddamn pretty.

                                        It was the
quickest way
                to get to Brooklyn, to be there
                when
she smiled.

                                                broke

                                                        bowed
his

                                                head
                his face   not

                        so much

                pretty now

                hurled

anxious   to [eve]r'   em   ember   's

                        stolen wisdom
                                        hurled child

                                                        belong

                                                to
                hip   on
                        hope

                on stony streets

                                    hot coals

                                        in the middle

        of a boiling sea

                                        trouble

almost

            at the hour of

                                ourselves

                        part breath

        part   dark ache

                                        nobody talking
                                    but the sky outside
                            eyes are something forgotten
                                maybe somebody's kinK
                            the big chair, the big silence
                            curled quietly in the corner

                                the hopes, the hand strokes
                                    old restless living
                            I hum a song kept from the light
                            when light, bound to endure,
                                        fills the room

How many kinds you think there are?

      Kind of slow, white men
      Kind of lost, them white men
      A crazy man
      Every white man
      The world ain't praised

      Kind of blue, black man
      Kind of scared, them black men
      A crazy man, every black man
      The world ain't changed

             This isn't
           what you know

                     every healing owned by it:
                        an outstretched palm
          against the air and then against the roar

                      strange as it hits the air
         spilled too suddenly   that circle of light
                      and touched too extremely

                   very little rescued down there
                     land of indigo, a soul
                     under the sound

               heavy nest, scarred and swollen
                     and black eyes
                 glittering like coal

a long silence decided
a thoughtfulness I'd never seen before
a frightening little courage

say something good and true:
1. He played good music.
2. His eyes give out like strings of the guitar.

say something good and true:
1. He was my annoying little brother.
2. He was *my good*, annoying little brother. All that light in his face.

: *Never Dreamed You'd Leave* :

wanted you

                              to show me

how to look after

                    wanted you

to teach me

how to cook, to squeeze a nothing

                         would have loved you

                              to go

and come back to my wedding

and sing

                    but since

: Sonny's Sister :

My brother didn't call me on my birthday
Didn't nothing, didn't write, didn't ask
Nobody didn't tell me he's safe, didn't nothing

I told a class of kids I enjoy being teacher
Because it is like being a big sister
But my only brother didn't call

On my birthday—he forgot nothing—he didn't
He wanted to not call, he told me before
You are fake and it hurt because I was proud

This disconnect, my kindred curb, has seen
The white of a knife
Yield to self-incision

I know what ease it is to be guillotined
From family, from symmetry
       to bow to cold candled eyes

: GOOD HAIR CAN'T FIX :

out of dream   black blades
curtsy their naked knees and prayer

                                is a windchime

                 where   piano legs

carry me over shoulder
spiral

          stems

                             be thrill my halo!

                         black mantle flames

bunch me
      like a hem

the armor wished

                 they pride   they pre-juiced

         against growth's compass   *teethe*
            press until repressed   *split*
            their target made

        middled
        slapped
      sectioned
       tucked

                        be neutral

                                        make no question of comfort
                                                        with your
                                                        volume

she forgets
        what it's like to be wound
she scoops and scoops your texture
pins it to her temple like a toy gun
invents a tertiary catcall she insists
is only
a joke:
                        Can we trade?

                                        dare you arrive
                                        dare you escape
                                        dare you do nothing

        ain' you sad for all them limping,
        frail thorns?
                        you a gown of helical harp strings
                                steaming tar from which
                        azaleas blaze
                                labyrinth of intricate twists
                                onyx loops
                        pajama blouse of bedtime blades

lampshade waves blacker than   the blackest part of lonely space

you got headscarves better looking   than their Garden of Eden
 at twilight

     they mad
you dangerous
you field of what has   not been found out

     SKINNA   MAH   RINK
                         MAH 'DO
                              UP THE STREET
    HAIL MAH 'SELF
       E'RY   MIRROR   AH MEET

SLINGING
        BLACK-FIST-SPATULA
                     SLINGING

        BLACK-FIST-DRACULA

PROP THE ROOTS
                  AFRO SEE AFRO
                         SEE FAMILY
AFROCADABRA
WE NOD

: MIRAGE :

Some of us put our hand on the stove
Feeling pranky for precautious daughter
Some of us keep a spot for you
If I add up the excuses
Dollars for the amount of shit I
Ear defending you, I'd be debtless. Sole
Inheritance, a frail family tree that looks
Up from underneath;

Flicking a Splenda pack like a dime bag
With a baby brother holding a gang sign
On the counter next to the biscotti jar:
Alexa, play 'Violent Crimes' volume 8
Played 2, 196 times last year
People told me last week this track was
Ghostwritten. It doesn't matter who's
Holding the pen, he sings

: BROKEN SONNET FOR BROKEN TELEPHONE :

remember: they outlawed our literacy
my 2002 history book in high school
held together by 2 pages on African American slavery
1 paragraph on Indian Residential Schools
the moral hazard; the foul condition; and the noise
it be some difficult, copping future archives
and records of *the things whispered in dark bedrooms*
the things imagined *when there was nowhere else to go*
I want to document my Self in case they try to esc alt or brainwash
the proof of hard teeth I thorned my story
through and into the fucking sky!
slop in the forehead, lobes twitching, fume humiliation
we've invented only what hatred we spew
to ourselves while pointing at at at and out out out

: I Want That Money Too :

bankrupt
why do they care so much about the
way we go dead? give me my drug
of impulse and I will eavestrough
happily alone :   b a d
knowledge of good
kill me well as well

                                   : to keep me
depths I've leapt   corners I've clipped
baggies blue white rich fat spoiled leaked
suicide safe from forceful knock-
less entry | | conspires
if drug (control) they want
they make money off my coffin too

: SUNFLOWER SHELLS :

even caskets
crack even
you can't
split that peel
that pit
inside eats
love even

even love
eats inside
pit that
peel that split
can't you
even crack?
caskets even?

: *Where Do All the Black People Live?* :

on TV?

I (wish I) was (absent) impervious? oblivious? how much my girlhood
wanted to

look more like my dad   be on the other side of his apostrophe

what is it about woman

that shrinks my sophistication
calls my pussy my tits and cortexes fast & stale on dinner plates?

I rebel
look at me and my enormous proper(ties)

hear my name and all its homonyms

except   accept

except I never feel accepted in gated communities

accept being black and groomed

to be casted "exotic"   you're exceptional

: MILLION DOLLAR BILL :

a new york intersection / greasy july afternoon / humid with sharks /
venture capitalists chief execs and saviors / two days / from gospel and
tall as a zebra / her collarbone cleft like tawny lilac tree / you could see
some of her / some dignity / creasing her / dress / from his corner office
/ a white man / with all the money and slaves / sees Whitney Houston and
says / *I want* / *get me* / *that*

because in my world / black women are always / discovered / and never
seen / until / they find each other / in my head of heads / I am waiting / for
some old guy / to discover me

pat me please / help me / please / there have been a few / one or two / one
put me in his audi / said we have business / meetings / I got a book on
branding and his hand / my thigh / another time he said ask me / for
anything / and put my framed head on his / desk / for a whole year / like a
souvenir / like a big catch

b. 1987 mid-November
Why is a member of the Nov not the ninth month?

Astro-nuggets of spleen & star dirt
Valentine's make-up gesture

What's written in the cosmic debris vs what's hereditary or genetically modified

Yes, I love sex
but that's because I'm a Scorpio

I'm deeply thoughtful and good at massaging cuticles
but that's because I'm a hip-hop head. #HunnidsWeTouch

Most likely to sagittar-that-a$$-up. *I like the knife pendant what's its meaning?*
That I'm a bad bitch and I'll cut dumb bitches off like crosswalks

Are there laws where you are?
When law is criminal, what moral support?

Can Black liberation have hot pu$$y
or must we wait for one then rush to the other side right quick?

: *This Tongue* :

This tongue slicks the inner ear

And if I must, I clean with this
Mourn with this
I camouflage with this tongue
Keep bedside calamine lotion, dab blisters
Lift spliff smoke from waxy basements with this
Hail cabs back to sober canopies
Consider this   tongue graffiti, a small sculpture I saved
    in case someone cut into my lane
Lamp oil and turpentine with this tongue
Because I've got to be (blood)let out

: BLACK BALANCE :

I am only a portrait
when they practice their aquarium eyes
on my blackness

I might have spoke
but the shutter's flash froze my mouth
I am not the thought that counts

And the betrayal is not that I stick out
like a windswept umbrella
but that I appear invisible

Had I been born with all my tongues
I might have been preoccupied
with the warmth of some banality

I might have stopped to gaze the clouds
or found a profit
I could take for granted

But I leap across the page
the wall, the room, the globe
and somehow, I am only the barrier they build upon me?

Is this blackness too much?
Is this blackness real?
When I have attended their tables

I might have fractured the ceiling
with my lack of regard
for their heelprint of dominance

Why aim skyward
when what is hidden and ancient within me
is the will to live wide?

I funnel my fury that lives
within the voice within me
and feel its roar finding traction

like the wingspan of a railroad
zipping the cleavage
of a quarantined city

to puncture this portrait
to bloom what is alive in me unspoken
I must interfere with wonder:

Had my ancestors been given today's future
who might I have been?
Between red margins

and white edge of page
I flicker my rage
and fix my aperture back at you

We don't have to touch
for you to recognize my betrayal as your own
We do this to each other

This anger can poison
or it can invent new songs of poise
Against the hum of history

I will arrive
and I will not live without language or luggage
any less precise

I meet you to recover
the dream not deferred but survived
behind every black poet's pen, behind every black painter's palette

every black musician's axe, and every
black photographer's eye
life giving life giving wide, wide life

: Is That How You Really Feel :

Yes, it's really weird to "stand on guard" before a flag
that didn't ask for me

If Jeff Bezos can make a thousand billion dollars, I want
all dollars discontinued

I want a national anthem written by Fefe Dobson
I want national anthems banned, *bands that make her dance*

Some asks ask too much

Like legalization of unadulterated cocaine
bought fair trade   shelved behind counters in drug-marts

I want more than one Black prof
More than one Black chance
More than one Black Prime Minister
More than one Black time of year
More than one Black   More than one Black   More than one Black   More
than one Black   More than one Black   More than one Black   More than one
Black   More than one Black   More than one Black   More than one Black
        More than one Black   More than one Black   More than one Black
More than one Black   More than one Black   More than one Black   More
than one Black   More than one Black   More than one Black   More than one
Black   More than one Black   More than one Black   More than one Black
        More than one Black   More than one Black   More than one Black

: WAX & HALLOWE'EN :

we are free and unforgetful this summer
it was winter when we brushed
one thumb mine and one yours
this naked feels planets I'll never reach
I could burn hail and sleet and burst
a downpour, how heavy this held breath?
It was winter when we rumbled
patience, everything patient and languid
in my pulse saying sit up, speak needles
I rush to the streetlamp addicted
and your hat-brim-umbrella sieves the

life-like fears and unfairness that
could skip overhead like flat river rocks
from your shoulder strap into your purse
a small collision that would travel lonely
until softer shadows quake lyrical
synapse, wordless as a rabbit foot
I want to keep you around for good
and no, we've never coupled
never have I held your nape in my hands
tie yourself to my tree, don't bye me
remind me every curse you said

: SHE COULD READ YOU :

She could read you to vapour

You wanted that phase beyond cloud
to close this small space
of untouched betrayal

You could end all legibility
And then imagine life afterkiss

Could she confiscate your obscurities?

You wanted to be felled
Onto
Into
Unto
Be felled
Onto
Into
Unto
Be felled
Onto
Into
Unto
Be felled
You wanted to be felt

: A GIRL'S BIKE :

First Sandy had the bike
A whole summer passed
Before Sandy found Angie on the bike
Some nights
A spin

We all saw Angie with the bike
and thought of Creamsicles
Then Sandy disappeared, stopped picking up the phone

Across the courtyard, I saw Sandy
The bike pulled her along
She couldn't stop to wave

When Angie got the bike for good
the chain came loose and loose and loose
She'd leave parties in tears and weeks later
We see the bike on Kijiji

I took the bike
Woke up with creamy blue skies
Shook beach grass from my hair and rode home

Sometimes past Angie or Sandy's house
I'd ride a risk
And was troubled not ever

I grew dizzy with Sandy and the bike with fourteen gears
"Best bike of my life!"
Sandy's small realities upset her

Now tell her how I know
The bike: one speed, the way
Those two or three summers go

begin this freedom
with my fingertips on the curve
where edges meet

backpedal birthmarks to homeland
and my body peels awake   to avoid ache
begin this freedom of femininity

how sapphire sweet my navel
intuitively speaks,   she warns me:
to be the woman I admire

I must admire myself, generously
but especially at my borders

I made a ritual of shining my mind, my mouth and ears
every day and instantly   I'm made every shade of majesty.

Giving myself permission to change
is a sort of freedom

if I desire more for myself
I become more of myself

believe this freedom quivers
with frightening affection

I fill into my body more than anybody

and value the girl I had to be in order to become
a better woman.

Here's any woman to fear and envy, that woman

with every tradition
I am
flood & fossil

equal parts permission and possibility

handsome thoughts in my head
and a book of ambitious bitches in my hand.

: *Dear Young Woman Echoes* :

         don't   live
the violence

more inner kindness

more

: Born Artist Maybe Not :

Every new

mnemonic tool or password I learn for power
systems have all been curtain called:

my mother's oppressive hover
my brother's distant deoxyribonucleic asterisk

my father's ability to take head count
before he's ever entered the room.

           Ain't I patterned
by numbers too?

My stable dining room table statistic:
three times a day I prefer blank

pages and TV formula. I got too used to learning
my part alone in locker rooms.

Does emptiness include
a first-class couple that fucked

with each other's credit scores.
Does emptiness ever stop thawing?   Ever uproot?

Where do I land

and how. do. we. fix our self-portraits
our prelude   our first bruise   our thick

and trained hair, our warped obedience. What happens
to harmony when it stops hitting

the rewind button on voicemails? Should I mourn
my grandmother's missing

when without grandmother home, I'm   alive?
Why am I the only one in my

corner with my last name. Was I not
blood enough? Was I too water?

I was water too. I watered the power outlets
that littered my life   my childhood is family room

heat, for—It never mattered
where I came from, by whom I survived

In what order do I breathe
count and matter?

: BIT :

In lieu of flowers I made language
my blood & my best friend
is a hardback diary, asking for arms
around a wound.
Or now, a fridge door
opened with my left hand
like the way I coil my fist or
pull someone back from traffic.
Below my cellophane bark,
I am an earth of ears begging for eyelids.
A strung climax when brains blow
and all is left are lights. Or, a lava lamp
gushing with cursive words
from my grandmother's homemade scripture book
& the megaphones thickening the walls
on school nights. Consider, then,
the four-year-old who draws an arrow
so she can flicker the noise & keep her mouth.
Thriving is the system
of those purple stalks spooning some
epiphanies to themselves.
Or, the sewing machine's needle,
paddling rejection & caterpillar fuzz.
I gave my voice the wingspan of a year.
I made myself out of basic cable
& a decent time alone. I made myself pretend
the ink I carried was the difference
between a vessel of piss & promise.
The bit I need, the fog around my ankles.

You are so close to my shape
I can feel you in my droop.
The fog around my ankles, the bit.

Notes

: *'s Back Again* :
The line *too fast, too soon* is nodding to Boyz II Men's song "Motownphilly".
Their lyrics are "Not too hard, not too soft."

: *Broken Sonnet for Broken Telephone* :
The italicized words are taken from Saidiya Hartman's piece in *The New Yorker* called "An Unnamed Girl, a Speculative History."

: *Cuffs or Halo* :
The poem is an ekphrasis responding to Taha Muharuma's photograph *And One.*

: *Good Hair Can't Fix* :
The capitalized words nod to musical group Sharon, Lois & Bram's song "Skinnamarink." The song is most notably recognized as the outro for the Canadian children's TV show called *The Elephant Show.*

: *Never Dreamed You'd Leave* :
The title is after Stevie Wonder's song "Never Dreamed You'd Leave in Summer." The poem nods to much of the song's lament.

: *Sonny's Found Poems* :
These poems were first built as erasures from the pages of James Baldwin's short story "Sonny's Blues" and then transferred to the blank page as found poems. The poems may appear with altered shapes, however, I attempted to maintain the integrity of the text found from each respective page as much as possible.

: Wires That Sputter :

The phrase *you stanza together* is inspired by Layli Long Soldier's work in her book *Whereas*, specifically her poem "Left."

The line *your bully and your craft* is after Carrianne Leung's piece "Coming to Voice." The original line is "So you see, silence is many things—both our oppressor and our craft."

The line "the light of the ear" is taken from a lecture given by Nathaniel Mackey called "Breath and Precarity" found on YouTube.

Acknowledgements

Give thanks to unseen, unknown forces. To hometowns not defined by geography but by other states, some I wish not to return to but am grateful to have lived through.

To you, reader. Thank you for considering this work, opening these pages to a bit of your life.

Endless love to Gilad, my husband and best friend. Whatcha doing, Bobby? I am privileged to have you as my support system: thanks for making coffees and dinners; for taking care of me and Toby; for always being down to leave the house, city, the country. You bring the best out of me.

To my high school basketball coach, Andrea Blackwell: your influence is unwavering. To my teachers, especially Mrs. Hefford, my grade 5 teacher. Something clicked when you wrote "poetry" on the chalkboard.

To the poets who helped me realize my earliest milestones in my career as a spoken word poet: Carlos Andrés Gómez, d'bi.young anitafrika, Michael Geffner, Dwayne Morgan, Alessandra Naccarato, and Tawhida Tanya Evanson. There's a rule-break here for every one of you.

To my Toronto Poetry Slam teammates and TPP community. To the poets, artists, and writers that recommend me for the type of opportunities that pay the bills and keep the lights on.

I am grateful to the many libraries, classrooms, gymnasiums, schools, arts organizations, and arts organizers that made it possible for me to lead workshops, mentor emerging artists, perform showcases, and share early drafts of some of these poems. To my mentees and the next generation of poets, I'll keep saying this: read twice as much as you write.

To my classmates and writing buddies in the Guelph MFA poetry workshop. Floating and thinking with you provided much luminosity in the drafting of this work. To Leanne Toshiko Simpson, for every conversation but especially our first.

To Dionne Brand, whose attention and feedback is invaluable. Many of these poems began as notes I made in the margins while reading *The Blue Clerk* and *No Language is Neutral*; on my first day of Professor Brand's poetry workshop I heard, "This is an advanced poetics class." What I would give to be back there, with all my advancements. Dionne, thank you for lending me your library.

To Canisia Lubrin, who granted me the gall, humour, and permission to thrust all doors off their hinges. Thank you for sensing this collection before I could, offering music and reading lists that continue to shape my literary education, and generous editing notes which I reread over and over—I am extremely grateful for every ounce of "good heat" you help me gain.

Utmost thanks to the team at McClelland & Stewart, particularly to Kelly Joseph and Chimedum Ohaegbu for all the exclamation marks (!!!) and making the publishing process fun at every stage. To Blossom Thom for proofreading and Talia Abramson for the book design.

To friends, old and new. To relatives, in-laws and immediate family; my parents and my brother Desmond. Mom, thank you for teaching me how to read and write and speak confidently. Love to Nanny, for every handwritten note and answering machine message.

This book is dedicated in loving memory of my grandmother, Mary Williams, and my cousin Chiquita "Quita" Adams: your voices are greatly missed but not nearly forgotten.